THE VALUE OF COURAGE

The Story of Jackie Robinson

SMACK

ILLUSTRATED BY
Pileggi

VALUE COMMUNICATIONS, INC.
PUBLISHERS
LA JOLLA, CALIFORNIA

THE VALUE OF COURAGE

The Story of
Jackie Robinson

BY SPENCER JOHNSON, M.D.

THE DANBURY PRESS

The Value of Courage is part of the ValueTale series.

The Value of Courage text copyright ©1977 by Spencer
Johnson, M.D. Illustrations copyright ©1977 by Value
Communications, Inc.

First Edition
Manufactured in the United States of America
For further information write to: ValueTales, P.O. Box 1012,
La Jolla, CA 92038

Library of Congress Cataloging in Publication Data

Johnson, Spencer.
    The value of courage.

    (ValueTales)
    SUMMARY: A biography, stressing the courage, of the
first black player in professional baseball.
    1. Robinson, John Roosevelt, 1919-1972—Juvenile
literature. 2. Baseball players—United States—
Biography—Juvenile literature. [1. Robinson, John
Roosevelt, 1919-1972. 2. Baseball players. 3. Afro-
Americans—Biography. 4. Courage]
I. Title.
GV865.R6J64   796.357'092'4 [B]   77-8865

ISBN 0-916392-12-0

For my wife Ann who has helped me
to understand the value of courage

This tale is about the courageous Jackie
Robinson. The story that follows is based on
events in his life. More historical facts about
Jackie Robinson can be found on page 63.

6

Once upon a time...

there lived a young boy named Jackie Robinson. Looking at him you might think he was just an ordinary boy. He walked like his friends. He talked like his friends. He even dressed like his friends.

But there was one thing about Jackie that made him very special. Can you guess what it was?

Jackie could run faster, jump higher, and throw a ball harder than anyone on the block.

"Hey, Jackie! Slow down!" his friends shouted. "We can't keep up with you!"

Jackie laughed. "This is as slow as I go!" he'd say. Then he would zip off over walls and around fences, running as if his shoes were on fire.

But Jackie didn't have much time for play. His family was poor and Jackie worked to help out. He delivered newspapers after school. And on weekends Jackie sold hot dogs at a baseball stadium near his home in California.

Jackie worked hard and sold lots of hot dogs. Of course he watched the ball games too, when he got the chance. One day as he watched Jackie noticed something. It was something he had seen before, but had never really thought about.

He looked at the pitcher and at the catcher. He looked at the batter and at the first baseman. He looked at the dugouts where the other players were sitting.

10

"I don't understand it," he said to himself. "There aren't any black players on either team."

"Hey, boy!" a man shouted. "How about one of those hot dogs?" Jackie jumped, and he hurried back to work.

That evening at supper Jackie asked, "Mama, how come blacks don't play on big league baseball teams? Aren't they good enough players?"

"Oh, they play well enough, Jackie," his mother answered. "But they aren't *allowed* to play in the big leagues. Only white men are allowed to play."

His brother Mack poked Jackie in the ribs, "They're afraid our color might rub off on them." Everyone but Jackie laughed, but at the same time they felt a little sad.

Jackie was angry. "That's not fair!"

His mother said. "No, I don't suppose it is. But you must control your temper. It's one thing to be brave. It's another to have courage."

Jackie didn't really know what that meant—at least not yet anyway. But he knew how he felt.

Jackie felt angry. "If somebody tried to stop *me*, I'd wrestle him to the ground!" Then he wrestled his favorite brother Mack to the floor to show what he meant.

Jackie's temper always got the better of him when it came to unfairness. But his mother understood. "Someday it might change," she said, "but not by fighting with your brother. Now finish your dinner, because I have a surprise for you."

What do you suppose the surprise was?

It was a baseball!

Oh, it wasn't the kind of a baseball that you can buy in a store. It was a ragball. Jackie's mother had made it out of woolen socks and bits of brightly colored cloth. She had tied it up with a bit of string and a lot of love.

When Jackie saw that ragball he let out a yell that rattled the windows. "My own baseball!" he shouted happily. "I'll keep it as long as I live!"

After that Jackie played with his ragball whenever he wasn't working or at school. He came to love the ragball so much that he even talked to it. He threw it high against brick walls. Then he caught it before it could fall back to the ground. "Gotcha!" he said. Then he tossed the ball against curbs and grabbed it as it bounced back to him. Jackie had a lot of fun playing with his ragball. They were as close as peanut butter and jelly.

Sometimes Jackie made believe he was a big league baseball player. He used to hit his ragball with a stick and pretend he was hitting a real baseball with a real bat.

But one day Jackie hit the ragball too hard. It flew up and up and up into the air.

And what do you think happened then?

17

The ragball split apart. Bits and pieces of colored cloth exploded out of it and scattered everywhere!

Jackie was heartbroken. "I've killed it!" he wept.

But then he thought he heard a strange little voice. "Don't cry, Jackie," the voice said. "I'm okay!"

Jackie blinked. Suddenly it *seemed* to him that his ragball was back in one piece again—and it was talking to him!

"My name is Rags," the ball seemed to say. "I'd like to be your best friend."

Jackie knew that his ragball was really in little bits and pieces and that it couldn't talk. And of course he knew that your best friend is yourself. When Jackie thought he was listening to Rags, he was really listening to his own thoughts.

"Well, Rags," Jackie said, "I can't think of a better friend to have."

With that, Jackie went home—and he pretended that Rags went along with him.

As Jackie grew up he liked to think that Rags went everywhere with him. Rags went along to help him on his jobs. Rags was with him when he practiced his favorite sports. When he practiced so much that his whole body ached, Rags always whispered good things to Jackie.

"Have courage, Jackie," Rags seemed to say, "and nothing can stop you. Remember that having courage is doing things that are hard to do—even things that you're afraid to do."

JOHN MUIR
TECH. H.S.

"Do you remember the Pepper Street gang?" asked Rags once. Jackie remembered well the boys he had known near his home on Pepper Street.

"Remember how easy it would have been to stay with the gang," Rags said. "And if you had stayed, you might now be stealing and lying like some of the others. If you had done what was easy then you'd probably be in big trouble now."

Jackie nodded. "It was *hard* to leave the gang," he admitted.

Rags added quickly, "It took courage for you to leave, but I'm glad you did." Jackie felt good. It was great to be together with Rags.

When Jackie was older he went to college at UCLA—the University of California at Los Angeles—where he became a star athlete. He was the first person in the history of the school to win sports awards in basketball, football, baseball, and track, all in the same year.

"What a great athlete!" said the fans who watched Jackie play.

One person who always rooted for Jackie was a girl named Rachel. Jackie really liked Rachel. He liked her so much that he asked her to be his girlfriend.

But not everyone cheered for Jackie. Some people tried to bully him because he was black. They called him a troublemaker when he got angry and stood up to them.

"Don't you know blacks shouldn't talk back?" sneered one man.

"Don't you know I'm a person, just like you?" replied Jackie angrily. "I'll say what I want and I'll do what I think is right!"

Rachel was proud of Jackie when he spoke up this way.

But Jackie tried not to worry when people said cruel things to him. He had more serious problems. "I'm going to have to quit school," he told Rags one day.

"Quit school?" cried Rags. "You can't! It's too important!"

"I know, but my mother just can't afford to keep me in school," said Jackie. "I have to get a job."

If you were a terrific athlete like Jackie, what kind of a job would you get?

27

That's right! You'd probably get a job in sports.

Jackie began getting paid to play professional football. He was a very, very good player. But he didn't stay with the football team long.

Do you know why?

Jackie quit football in order to join the army. Like most people, Jackie didn't want to go to war. But the United States had declared war and Jackie wanted to help his country.

He was a good soldier, but he found a lot of unfairness even in the army. One day when he wanted to ride on a bus, he found out how unfair some people could be. Something happened that was very common in those days.

Do you have any idea what it was?

After Jackie got on the bus and sat down, the bus driver yelled at him. "Hey, black man," he said, "get to the back of the bus where you belong!"

"I will not," said Jackie. "I'll sit up front just like anybody else." And Jackie stayed in the front of the bus, not budging from where he had sat. Some of the passengers didn't like this. They felt that only white people were good enough to sit up front. They even tried to get Jackie in trouble. But he had the courage to do what he knew was right.

"Atta boy, Jackie!" cried Rags. "I'm proud of you!"

Jackie was proud, too. And he was glad when the whole thing finally turned out all right. But deep down inside, he was sad. "How can some people be so unfair to other people?" he whispered to Rags.

Of course after Jackie finally got out of the army he needed a job again. And of course the first thing he thought of was sports.

"Why not try baseball?" said Rags. "They don't allow black athletes to play in the big leagues, but you could play for the Negro American League."

Jackie decided to try it. He went to Kansas City and joined the Monarchs, an all-black baseball team. "If this works out," he thought, "Rachel and I can get married soon."

After Jackie had been with the Kansas City Monarchs awhile, people began talking about what a terrific player he was. Sportswriters began turning out stories about the way he could hit and run, throw and catch.

And, while Jackie was playing for the Monarchs, an important man who lived faraway was also talking about him.

Who do you think the man was, and what do you think he was saying?

The man was Branch Rickey. He lived in New York and was president of the Brooklyn Dodgers, a famous big league baseball team.

"Lots of black people are darn good athletes," Branch Rickey said to a friend. "It's about time that a black man gets a chance to play baseball in the major leagues. And from what you tell me, Jackie Robinson is the best black baseball player there is. I'm going to ask him to play on one of our try-out baseball teams, the one in Montreal."

Branch Rickey knew he'd be criticized for hiring a black player. It took courage, but he sent for Jackie anyway.

Soon after Jackie arrived at Mr. Rickey's office, he was asked a difficult question.

"I want to know one thing," he said to Jackie. "Can you play the game, no matter how ugly and mean some people are to you? Will you be able to take it without losing your temper?"

"Mr. Rickey," said Jackie, "are you looking for a black man who's afraid to fight back?"

Branch Rickey shook his head. "No. I'm looking for a ball player with courage enough *not* to fight back."

Jackie understood. Some of the white players would try to make him quit. They'd throw baseballs at him. They'd step on him with spiked shoes. They'd call him ugly names. They'd do anything to prove that blacks weren't good enough for big league baseball. Jackie would have to take it. He would not be able to fight back, because if he did, he could ruin the chances of other blacks to play big league baseball.

"It will be hard," Mr. Rickey warned, "and it will take a lot of courage."

Jackie nodded. "I'll try, Mr. Rickey," he said. Then he and Branch Rickey shook hands.

"Jackie, do you have a special friend?" Branch
Rickey asked.

"I sure do," said Jackie. "She's a great girl, and her
name is Rachel."

"Good," said Mr. Rickey. "A great girl is hard to
find, and you're going to need all the help you can get."

"We plan to get married as soon as we can," said Jackie.

So Jackie and Rachel were married. Jackie was glad
to have Rachel and her warmth and wisdom with
him when he left for his first game in Montreal.

When Jackie arrived in Montreal Rags was also with him. Rags was always around when Jackie was nervous or upset.

"What if I don't play well enough?" Jackie asked Rags. "This is just a try-out team. If I'm not good enough I won't get to New York and I won't play for the Brooklyn Dodgers."

"You're as good as any player here," said Rags.

"But I've got to be *better* than any player here," said Jackie.

Rags laughed, "Then *be* better!"

Jackie *was* better. He hit the ball hard. He caught the ball practically every time. He even stole a few bases. He didn't pay any attention when some players on other teams yelled at him and called him dirty names.

Then one day the players on another team did something awful!

They threw a black cat out onto the playing field and yelled, "Hey! Jackie Robinson! Here's your cousin! He's black too!"

Jackie's stomach tightened up. His fists clenched. He wanted to fight.

"Careful!" whispered Rags. "You know what Mr. Rickey told you. And remember what your mother said long ago. It's one thing to be brave and to be willing to fight back. But it's another to have courage to do what's hard and *not* fight back."

Jackie thought for a minute, then he did the thing that was so difficult for him. He calmed down and refused to fight.

The other men were mad when they saw that they couldn't make Jackie lose his temper. They knew if Jackie stayed calm, he would play even better—*against them*!

41

He did play better. In fact, he played so well that after only one year with the Montreal team Branch Rickey called him and said, "I want you and Rachel to come to New York. You're going to play for the Brooklyn Dodgers."

Those were the words Jackie had been waiting to hear. He wanted to tell Rachel the good news right away. But he was a little worried too. "I wonder what will happen to me in New York?" he said to Rags.

One thing that happened was that Jackie's picture was in many of the New York newspapers. In those days, even some of the sportswriters believed that there wasn't a black man in the country who was good enough for the big leagues. "Jackie Robinson will fail," said some of the newspaper articles.

Jackie sighed. "How can I play well, when so many people want me to fail just because I'm black?"

But before he knew it, Jackie was in a Dodger uniform, ready for his first big league game.

The first game was about to begin. The Dodgers came onto the field. Jackie tossed a grounder to Pee Wee Reese, the great Dodger shortstop. Pee Wee scooped up the ball and flipped it to Eddie Stanky, the second baseman. Eddie then threw the ball to Jackie. Jackie felt the ball thump into his mitt. It was a simple catch, but a trickle of sweat rolled down the back of Jackie's neck. His heart beat faster, and his hand felt damp inside his mitt. Jackie knew that his palms were sweating. He was very nervous!

Then he heard ugly words. "Hey, black boy!" someone shouted. "You don't belong here. Get off the field!"

"So you're Jackie Robinson," someone from the other team yelled. "We'll show you that you can't play in the big leagues."

Jackie's teammates just watched and listened. They didn't try to defend Jackie, even though he was on their team.

Somehow Jackie managed to ignore the shouts and the insults. He played all right when the game finally started. And for a few more games he played very well. But then it happened!

Jackie's courage began to weaken. He felt the anger of the fans. He heard their boos and the shouts. He still wanted to do well for Branch Rickey, for his team, and for other blacks who wanted to get into the major leagues. And, of course, for himself. But it seemed too hard. Like everyone else does at times, he was giving up. He began to play badly. In game after game he failed to hit the ball.

"See!" said one of the players on the other team. "I told you black people aren't any good at baseball!"

During one very bad game, Jackie sat sadly in the dugout. "Everybody seems to be against me," he sighed. "I feel all alone."

"I know you do, Jackie," whispered Rags, "but having courage means seeing things through. No matter how hard it is, you've got to keep trying. Besides, you never know what might happen."

The next game began badly. Some fans shouted at Jackie. Players on the other team yelled insults. As usual, the men on Jackie's team did nothing to help Jackie.

But then a very unexpected thing happened. Almost everyone in the stadium saw it. The great Dodger player, Pee Wee Reese, walked over, put his arm around Jackie's shoulder, and said, "We're with you, Jackie." He knew how hard it was for Jackie to be the only black player in the major leagues.

At last Jackie had found a real teammate.

Now he was more determined than ever to play his best—no matter how hard it was.

Jackie came to bat. The pitcher threw the ball. An instant later the stadium echoed to the sound of a loud crack! Jackie had hit the ball into the outfield for a double!

Jackie played well for the rest of the day—and for many days after that. Gradually most of the fans and players stopped booing and insulting him.

There was, however, at least one player who still wanted to hurt Jackie. And he planned to do it soon.

Without warning, a big player from the other team charged at Jackie like a wild bull. He cut Jackie with his spiked shoes. Jackie began to bleed.

Without thinking, Jackie Robinson clenched his fists, ready to fight.

"No," screamed Rags. "That would be too easy."

Jackie took a deep breath and relaxed his hands. Soon he was surrounded by his teammates, who helped him as he limped off the field.

His teammates knew, and even the fans who read the newspapers knew, that it was Jackie's nature to fight back. It must have taken a lot of courage for Jackie not to hit the other player.

"Jackie's done it," Mr. Rickey told Rachel. "He's shown he's got courage when it's needed most."

Rachel couldn't know it that day, but Jackie's courage was going to change big league baseball completely. And Rachel was going to see the change with her own eyes.

What do you think Rachel saw?

As time went by, Rachel saw more and more black athletes on big league playing fields.

Jackie had done what he had set out to do. His courage had led the way. Now everyone knew that a good player was a valuable addition to a team, whether that player was black or white.

Rags was so proud that he hardly knew what to do with himself. "Jackie," he said, "you've helped all black athletes, and you've won just about every major award a baseball player can win!"

Jackie laughed. "I know. But I'm happiest because I helped the Brooklyn Dodgers win their first championship of the world."

Eventually Jackie gave up playing baseball. What do you think he did next?

Jackie Robinson became a spokesman for the rights of black people. He talked to groups of people all over the country.

"It's time everyone treated black people as equals," Jackie said. "I know that things are getting a little better, but they have to get much better, and *very* soon!"

Some people didn't like to hear Jackie reminding them of how really unfair they were to black people. They didn't want to think about it, but Jackie *made* them think about it. He had the courage to say what was right, no matter what happened. Most people admired Jackie for his courage.

Rags was happy that Jackie could now speak out for the rights of black people. Jackie didn't know it yet, but one of the happiest days for him was yet to come.

Several years after he stopped playing, Jackie was given the highest honor a baseball player can receive. He was voted into the Baseball Hall of Fame.

Many of the greatest baseball players of all time were there to show how much they respected Jackie. So were some of our country's highest leaders. As he listened to them cheering for him, Jackie's eyes filled with happy tears.

Then Jackie heard a small voice whispering to him. "No one deserves this honor more than you," said Rags. "You earned it because of your great courage."

And what about you? Is there something that's very hard for you to do? Maybe it's even something you're afraid of. Well, are you going to have the courage to do it?

You may not become one of the greatest baseball players of all time, but you can do something *just* as important.

You can learn the value of courage by doing what is *hard* for you to do. Then *you* can be happier too, just like our courageous friend Jackie Robinson.

The End

John Roosevelt (Jackie) Robinson was born in Cairo, Georgia in 1919, the youngest of five children. His sharecropper father abandoned the family six months after Jackie was born. Despite a lack of money, Jackie's mother was determined to find a better life for her children and moved her family to California when Jackie was only sixteen months old.

Jackie and his brothers Edgar, Frank, and Mack, and his sister Willa Mae, grew up on Pepper Street in Pasadena, California. Their mother Mallie supported her family by working at various domestic jobs. Jackie remembered his mother with pride: "I thought she must have some kind of magic to be able to do all the things she did, to work so hard and never complain and to make us all feel happy."

At one point in his youth, Jackie began to run with a neighborhood gang. An older friend made Jackie realize how much he was hurting his mother as well as himself. As Jackie later said, "He told me that it didn't take guts to follow the crowd, that courage and intelligence lay in being willing to be different." Jackie listened and left the gang.

As he grew up, Jackie developed into a sensational athlete. He starred in football, basketball, baseball, and track. He attended UCLA where he became the first person ever to win athletic awards (letters) in all four sports.

Jackie left UCLA in 1941 and began playing professional football with the Los Angeles Bulldogs. World War II cut short his football career. He served in the army for thirty-one months and was discharged as a first lieutenant.

He made his professional baseball debut in 1945 with the Monarchs of the Negro American Baseball League. His abilities as a player brought him to the attention of Branch Rickey, president of the Brooklyn Dodgers baseball team. Rickey, in what was an act of great courage at the time, had decided to break the color barrier which then existed in major league baseball. Jackie was signed to play for the Dodgers' top minor league team, the Montreal Royals, for the 1946 season.

JACKIE ROBINSON
1919–1972

In 1947 Rickey moved Jackie to the Dodgers. Despite the tremendous pressure of being the first black baseball player in the major leagues, Jackie played outstanding baseball and was voted rookie of the year. His best year was 1949 when he led the league in hitting and was voted its most valuable player. Jackie played for the Dodgers for ten years during which they won the National League title six times. In 1955 it was Jackie's spectacular play that led to the Dodgers' first World Series Championship. He retired from baseball after the 1956 season.

Jackie, even as a young person, was an outspoken black man. He was in many ways ahead of his times. Many people did not like his comments on racial injustice. However, he had the courage to speak his mind in public on what he believed to be the rights of blacks.

Jackie shared the pains and joys of his life with his wife Rachel, whom he married in 1946. Rachel was a source of considerable strength for him.

In later life Jackie Robinson suffered quietly from the pains of diabetes. He died from diabetic complications in 1972. But even now his life story continues to act as an outstanding example of the value of courage.

Other Titles in the ValueTale Series

THE VALUE OF BELIEVING IN YOURSELF	The Story of Louis Pasteur
THE VALUE OF DETERMINATION	The Story of Helen Keller
THE VALUE OF PATIENCE	The Story of the Wright Brothers
THE VALUE OF KINDNESS	The Story of Elizabeth Fry
THE VALUE OF HUMOR	The Story of Will Rogers
THE VALUE OF TRUTH AND TRUST	The Story of Cochise
THE VALUE OF CARING	The Story of Eleanor Roosevelt
THE VALUE OF CURIOSITY	The Story of Christopher Columbus
THE VALUE OF RESPECT	The Story of Abraham Lincoln
THE VALUE OF IMAGINATION	The Story of Charles Dickens
THE VALUE OF FAIRNESS	The Story of Nellie Bly
THE VALUE OF SAVING	The Story of Benjamin Franklin
THE VALUE OF LEARNING	The Story of Marie Curie
THE VALUE OF SHARING	The Story of the Mayo Brothers
THE VALUE OF RESPONSIBILITY	The Story of Ralph Bunche
THE VALUE OF HONESTY	The Story of Confucius
THE VALUE OF GIVING	The Story of Ludwig van Beethoven
THE VALUE OF UNDERSTANDING	The Story of Margaret Mead
THE VALUE OF LOVE	The Story of Johnny Appleseed
THE VALUE OF FANTASY	The Story of Hans Christian Andersen
THE VALUE OF FORESIGHT	The Story of Thomas Jefferson
THE VALUE OF HELPING	The Story of Harriet Tubman
THE VALUE OF DEDICATION	The Story of Albert Schweitzer
THE VALUE OF FRIENDSHIP	The Story of Jane Addams
THE VALUE OF ADVENTURE	The Story of Sacagawea